Gender Equality

Sean Connolly

FRANKLIN WATTS
LONDON•SYDNEY

An Appleseed Editions book

First published in 2005 by Franklin Watts

Paperback edition 2007

Franklin Watts
338 Euston Road, London NW1 3BH

Franklin Watts Australia
Level 17/ 207 Kent Street, Sydney, NSW 2000

© 2005 Appleseed Editions

Appleseed Editions Ltd
Well House, Friars Hill, Guestling, East Sussex TN35 4ET

Designed by Helen James

ISBN 978 0 7496 7646 9 √√✗

Dewey Classification: 323.3' 4

A CIP catalogue for this book is available from the British Library

Photographs by Corbis (Archivo Iconografico, S.A., Bettmann, Stefano Bianchetti,
Andrew Brookes, Christie's Images, Laura Dwight, Historical Picture Archive,
Hulton–Deutsch Collection, Christel Gerstenberg, J. A. Giordano, Teru Kuwayama,
James Leynse, Jeff J Mitchell/Reuters, Reuters, Zach Seckler, Ariel Skelley, Christopher
Smith, Wendy Stone), Getty Images (Wathiq Khuzaie, HIROKO MASUIKE/AFP)

Printed in China

Franklin Watts is a division of Hachette Children's Books

Contents

Finding a Voice

One of the most important achievements in the past two centuries has been the development of **civil rights** for people who had been previously denied them. Many campaigns for such rights have been conducted side by side, with activists learning from each other's experiences. People in most countries now enjoy the freedom to worship as they please or to look for a job regardless of the colour of their skin or the language they speak. Powerful and united reform movements have swept away slavery and improved conditions for people with physical or mental disabilities.

The people who have benefited from such reforms have usually been **minority groups** – people who make up less (often far less) than half of a population. For example, African-Americans, who once faced slavery, make up about 10 per cent of the population in the United States. Catholics, who were once victims of **discrimination** in Northern Ireland, represent about 40 per cent of the total population there. Denying a smaller group some basic rights has, unfortunately, been common in world history.

Strength in Numbers?

Women, on the other hand, form at least half of the world's population. Yet for many centuries women had little or no independence and were required to obey either their fathers or their husbands. In many countries, women could not own property or businesses. Their children were considered the 'property' of their husband, even if he was cruel or had abandoned his wife. And to make matters worse, women did not have the right to improve their position by voting for changes in society.

Men based their control over women on social traditions that reflected men's physical strength and power. Many people interpreted religious texts in a way that justified poor treatment of women. And, with women in no real position to change things, these poor conditions continued for centuries even while men were developing new notions of freedom and democracy for themselves.

4

The struggle for women's rights continues in the disputed region of Kashmir, on the border between India and Pakistan, where many women seek shelter in refugee camps.

'My wish is to ride the tempest, tame the waves, kill the sharks. I will not resign myself to the usual lot of women who bow their heads and become concubines.'

Trieu Thi Trinh, peasant who led an insurrection against Chinese invaders of Vietnam, AD 240.

Ancient Equality

It is easy to believe that history has been moving constantly forwards and that people today enjoy more rights and equality than those who lived hundreds or even thousands of years ago. According to this view, modern women should be grateful for the advances of the last two centuries which overturned thousands of years of discrimination.

The truth, however, is very different. For example, women in many ancient societies enjoyed more basic rights than women in 19th-century England or the United States. The legal code of Hammurabi, drawn up in about 1700 BC in ancient Babylon, supported gender equality. A woman's land and other property remained her own throughout her marriage, and when she died they passed on to her children (not to her husband). A woman in ancient Egypt could even charge her husband **interest** on any money he borrowed from her! And in Sparta, the Greek city-state famed for its fierce warriors, women owned two-thirds of the land. European men first meeting the Iroquois – a Native American nation as warlike as the Spartans – were shocked to discover that women owned all of the houses and tools in each village.

A wall painting from the Valley of Kings depicts Queen Nefertiti, one of ancient Egypt's most famous rulers, in prayer.

Gradually, a number of brave women risked their position in society by calling for improvements to their own conditions. The campaign for gender equality started with a few stray voices but, with each generation, it gained new momentum and support. By the late 19th century, women were able to tap their 'strength in numbers' to drive home calls for change. But even then, activists met stiff resistance from both men and women.

At the beginning of the 21st century, the campaign for gender equality has achieved many stunning successes. Women have risen to positions of authority and respect in many countries. But the struggle continues in

some countries where customs and traditions still deny women any real equality. Poverty and **illiteracy** are the biggest enemies of those who want to promote gender equality, but this latest struggle has the example of other successes to guide it. It has become harder for countries to 'go it alone' and ignore world opinion. And this opinion has turned very much in favour of equality between girls and boys, women and men.

The modern world has seen a number of gender 'role reversals', including more men staying at home with children while their wives go to work.

'Extending over more than a century and including most nations of the globe, the cause of woman suffrage has been one of the great democratic forces in human history.'

Ellen Carol DuBois, American academic, 1989.

Birth of a Movement

Most of the societies that developed in the period known in Europe as the Middle Ages (beginning in about the sixth century AD) had clear-cut rules to define everyone's role. Powerful kings created some of these rules; others tied in with religious practice. For example, the Jewish and Christian faiths taught that the first woman, Eve, had to obey the first man, Adam. Christian wedding ceremonies called on wives to 'honour and obey' their husbands. This view was not limited to the **Western** world. The highest honour that a Hindu woman could achieve was to be **reincarnated** as a man in the next life.

Religious ceremonies, such as this 19th-century Russian wedding, often reinforced cultural notions of male and female roles.

'Women live like bats or owls, labour like beasts and die like worms.'

Duchess Margaret of Newcastle (England), 17th century.

New ways of thinking about the world began to develop in the 15th century. The Renaissance, a great artistic movement in Europe, recaptured the inspiration of ancient Greece and Rome to find new ways of representing the world. The spirit of **humanism**, which developed at the same time, celebrated human beauty and potential. And the Protestant faiths that developed at the time of the **Reformation** cast aside many Catholic traditions in order to place each worshipper in direct contact with God.

Unfortunately, none of these developments did much to improve the position of women in society. Later, with the rise of new thinking about democracy during the 18th-century **Age of Enlightenment** in Europe, many women believed that once again only men's lives would benefit.

Enlightenment thinkers such as Voltaire inspired many men – and women – to question the assumptions that denied women equality.

Revolutionary Ideas

The rush of new political ideas was confined to essays and pamphlets until the end of the 18th century, when two **revolutions** rocked the world. The American Revolution gave birth to the United States in 1776. In some ways, however, it was the French Revolution, beginning 13 years later, that sent more shock waves through the rest of the world. French writers, such as Voltaire and Jean-Jacques Rousseau, had been at the forefront of Enlightenment calls for freedom and equality. In 1789, their supporters had a chance to put these ideas into practice. Made desperate by the poor conditions faced by most people, the French public began to overthrow most of the political structure that had dominated their country.

Although women were at the forefront of the French Revolution, they ultimately did not gain equal rights as a result of the battle. But the ideas of equality that came from this struggle helped give women around the world a new voice. Women in England and other countries took up the cause, and the **feminist** movement was born.

'Woman is born free and her rights are the same as those of a man . . . The law must be an expression of the general will; all citizens, men and women alike, must participate in making it . . . it must be the same for all.'

From Olympe de Gouges's 'Declaration of the Rights of Women and Citizenesses', 1791.

Liberty Leading the People, *an 1830 painting by French artist Eugène Delacroix, used the image of Woman to symbolize the struggle for universal freedom.*

The Rights of Women

French revolutionaries filled the air of Paris with their hearty cries of 'Liberty, Brotherhood, and Equality'. This slogan seemed to sum up the goals and hopes of people in the new France. Early in the Revolution, the new government reflected these feelings with its 'Declaration of the Rights of Man'. But, despite the sweeping changes that this radical document promised, one thing remained much the same as it had been during the Old Regime – the position of women in society.

Some French women argued strongly for true equality, which would extend to women. In 1791, an actress named Olympe de Gouges (1748–93) published the 'Declaration of the Rights of Women and Citizenesses'. This document was intended to extend the new freedoms to women. 'Women, wake up!' de Gouges called. 'Recognize your rights!' Seeing the executions that accompanied the revolution, she stated that women should have the right to vote and be elected 'if they have the right to go to the **scaffold**'. This observation proved to be only too true for de Gouges. When divisions among revolutionaries developed into bloody violence, she lost her head at the **guillotine** in 1793.

There were, however, other people beyond France who were prepared to carry on the message of Olympe de Gouges. Mary Wollstonecraft (1759–97) was an English writer and translator who supported the democratic goals of the French Revolution and, in particular, de Gouges's writings. In 1792, Wollstonecraft published *A Vindication of the Rights of Woman*, in which she spelled out the inequalities that women continued to face and her proposals to overcome these injustices. The 300-page book became an instant bestseller, and its well-developed arguments became the foundation of the feminist movement.

'Women might also study politics and businesses of all kinds, if they were educated in a more orderly manner. How many women thus waste life away, who might have practised as physician, regulated a farm, managed a shop, and stood erect supported by their own industry, instead of hanging their heads?'

From Mary Wollstonecraft's *A Vindication of the Rights of Woman*, 1792.

Joining Forces

During the 19th century, the ideas that had developed in the 18th century spread rapidly. Breakthroughs in communications linked people in different parts of the world in ways that had seemed impossible just a few decades earlier. Railways and steamships spanned oceans and continents, while the telegraph gave people the ability to communicate instantly. Because of these advances, ideas flowed more easily from one country to another.

One of the great ideas was that of gender equality, or women's rights. The struggle for gender equality during the French Revolution had inspired women in other countries. The United States, itself only a few decades old and dedicated to liberty, offered fertile soil in which these ideas could take root. But the longstanding grievances of American women paled beside an even greater American injustice: slavery.

Reaching Out

American women were at the heart of the battle to end slavery in the United States. The antislavery movement, known as abolitionism, gained strength in the first decade of the 1800s. And the issue of slavery lay at the heart of the North-South dispute that tore the country apart during the Civil War (1861–65).

A 19th-century woman types a telegram. With the invention of the telegraph, news that had once taken days or months to reach its destination could be sent and received within minutes.

Education for Women

Before the 19th century, women had little hope of being educated to the same level as men. A lucky few from wealthy families received a private education, but most girls did not attend school for more than a few years. And the idea of further education at colleges and universities was out of the question. Things began to change in the 1830s. In 1833, Oberlin College was founded in Ohio, in America. It promised to educate women as well as men. It also became the first American college to offer places to African-Americans. Other colleges specifically for women were founded in the following years, including Girton College in England (1869). They were pioneers in offering first-class educational opportunities to women.

A female teacher in Manhattan, 1886. By the late 1800s, women had begun seizing the chance to educate themselves and others.

Reformers such as the British abolitionist William Wilberforce (1759–1833) concentrated on the 'peculiar institution', as slavery was called. Young and old, black and white, religious leaders and non-believers united to overthrow slavery. Female abolitionists saw that this unity gave the anti-slavery movement a wider appeal. They began to use its methods – including public speeches, sometimes before hostile crowds – in their own struggle to achieve equal rights for women.

By the 1840s, many women around the world were drawing the same conclusion – that women's inferior position in society would never change unless

And Ain't I a Woman?

One of the most courageous American women of the 19th century was Sojourner Truth (1797–1883), who escaped from slavery and became one of the most inspiring speakers of the abolitionist movement. Her difficult life and success in overcoming enormous obstacles made her an example to African-Americans and to women in general. Truth was a passionate supporter of women's rights and contributed her energy to the cause. In one of her most famous speeches, addressing a women's rights convention in 1851, she listed all of the hardships she had endured. After each of these, she cried, 'And ain't I a woman?' The effect was electrifying. Truth showed that with enough determination, a woman could work hard, put up with punishment, and cope with life's troubles just as well as any man could.

Sojourner Truth was already 46 when she first spoke publicly about slavery and women's rights, but she continued campaigning for four decades.

'Look at this arm! I have plowed and planted and gathered into barns, and no man could [better] me – and ain't I a woman? I could work as much and eat as much as any man – when I could get it – and bear the **lash** as well – and ain't I a woman?'

Sojourner Truth, speaking in 1851.

women united to make their voices heard. The British writer Harriet Martineau (1802–76), for example, combined a heartfelt opposition to slavery with calls for wider social equality generally. In London, at the world antislavery congress of 1840, American feminists Lucretia Coffin Mott (1793–1850) and Elizabeth Cady Stanton (1820–1906) were denied the right to speak because leading male speakers argued that women's rights were against God's will.

They were infuriated by this rebuff from people who were, in so many other ways, sensitive to equal rights. Over the next few years, they planned ways to help women to make their voices heard. The result was another milestone in the history of the struggle for gender equality – the Seneca Falls Declaration of 1848, agreed by the Women's Rights Convention (meeting at Seneca Falls, New York). The struggle took many forms around the world. A series of publicized British divorce cases highlighted the difficulties faced by British women seeking to end marriages with cruel or unfaithful husbands. Other women were even more degraded. The Australian Conciliator for the Aborigines found cases where Aboriginal girls and women had been taken by force from their families.

An engraving of the Seneca Falls Convention shows a delegate denouncing men while male onlookers in the balconies mock and cheer.

The Seneca Falls Declaration

American feminists had been deeply involved in the abolitionist movement in the early 19th century. But even among like-minded men who shared a view of social progress, women were forced to accept limited roles in the struggles. The humiliating experience of Lucretia Coffin Mott and Elizabeth Cady Stanton, who were virtually banned from an antislavery conference in London in 1840, was the last straw. The pair returned to the US intent on ensuring that their voices – and the women's rights message – would be heard.

Mott and Cady Stanton organized the first women's rights convention in July 1848. It was held in a small chapel in Seneca Falls, New York. The convention attracted between 100 and 300 people, including male supporters. Among this group was former slave Frederick Douglass, an important figure in the abolitionist movement. The Convention heard speakers discuss the injustices that women faced in every aspect of their lives. Many laws in the US – concerning land ownership, marriage, education and government – strengthened men's position at the expense of women.

'He has never permitted her to exercise her inalienable right to the elective franchise. . . . He has taken from her all right in property, even to the wage she earns . . . becoming to all intents and purposes, her master. . . .'

Some of man's injustices to woman, outlined in the Seneca Falls Declaration, 1848.

Cady Stanton drafted the Seneca Falls Declaration, in which she deliberately imitated the US Declaration of Independence. The convention approved the declaration as a statement of purpose for the movement as a whole, but public reaction was bitterly divided. Many leading thinkers, including Horace Greeley and William Lloyd Garrison, supported it strongly. Other people, and most American newspapers, criticized the declaration and mocked feminists for being unladylike and aggressive. Battle lines were drawn, and the debate was now in the open.

Support from Men

Women were not alone in their views about gender equality. Many of the feminists had supportive fathers or husbands. And men were influential in their own right in publicizing demands for equality.

English philosopher William Thompson wrote his *Appeal of One-half the Human Race, Women, Against the Pretensions of the Other Half, Men* in 1825. Another English philosopher, John Stuart Mill, published a famous essay, 'The **Subjugation** of Women', in 1869. Friedrich Engels, the co-founder of **communism**, saw women's inferior position as part of a wider political problem. In his 1889 book *The Origins of the Family, Private Property, and the State*, he argued that women in ancient societies had far more equality than women in his own time and that 19th-century women had been reduced to 'domestic servants'.

John Stuart Mill used his persuasive logic to argue for gender equality.

Elizabeth Cady Stanton insisted that just government could not exist without the consent of the governed.

'The history of all times, and of today especially, teaches that . . . women will be forgotten if they forget to think about themselves.'

Luise Otto-Peters, German feminist, 1849.

Campaigns to Vote

The Seneca Falls Declaration of 1848 echoed what most campaigners for gender equality had decided: women would never benefit from lasting change unless they had the power to create that change themselves. And in democratic societies, the power to create change can only come from having the right to vote. This right is also called suffrage.

Woman suffrage was one of the most hotly debated issues of the late 19th and early 20th centuries. It became central to the wider discussions of women's employment, education, marriage rights and property ownership. Suffragists, as supporters of woman suffrage became known, used a range of tactics to publicize their cause and to show their power once they were united.

American feminists were as pleased as any abolitionists when African-American men were granted the right to vote in 1870. That put black men – in the eyes of the law, if not of some racist Americans – on the same footing as white American men. But black and white women remained without a say in the democratically elected government. The same was true throughout

Women had the right to vote in several western states by the time these suffragists demonstrated in New York in 1912.

WE WERE VOTERS OUT WEST! WHY DENY OUR RIGHTS IN THE EAST?

the world; there was no country in the middle of the 19th century in which women had the same voting rights as men.

This 1908 illustration depicts the arrival in London of impassioned woman suffrage activists.

Same Cause, Different Approaches

The suffragist movement became divided – at times bitterly – over how best to press for women's rights, especially the right to vote. The British Reform Bill of 1832 widened the rights of men but seemed to lock women in a weak position. Some radical feminists believed that sweeping changes were needed immediately. Maria Desraimes, the founder of the first Society for Women's Rights in 1866, turned the religious issue on its head by attacking the Church as being part of the problem in keeping women in an inferior state. Others in Europe urged compromise as the only way forward. A third way, exemplified by the famously unmarried Florence Nightingale, was to keep away from the snares of dealing with men – and the risk of becoming their 'property'.

An International Movement

The issue of woman suffrage and gender equality was not confined to the English-speaking world. Pandita Ramabai (1858–1922), a Hindu scholar from India, travelled around her country establishing women's organizations. Kishida Toshiko (1863–1901) was a leader in the Japanese woman suffrage movement. Raden Ajen Kartini (1879–1904) was a passionate supporter of women's rights in Indonesia. Chinese suffragists united in 1911 to form the Chinese Suffragette Society. They led public demonstrations to picket meetings of the Chinese National Assembly as part of their campaign for woman suffrage.

New York's The Daily Graphic *ran this caricature of Susan B. Anthony under the title 'The Woman Who Dared' before her 1873 trial.*

Americans differed dramatically on the issue of whether women should be granted the right to vote at the same time as African-American men. Organizations representing these rival views were set up in 1869. Elizabeth Cady Stanton and Susan B. Anthony established the National Woman Suffrage Association to work for a national change. Lucy Stone and Henry Ward Beecher – who feared that the abolitionist cause would suffer if women were too extreme – founded the American Woman Suffrage Association. Both groups soon achieved notable publicity. The **territory** of Wyoming granted women the right to vote in 1869 and, in 1872, Susan B. Anthony led a group of women to vote in an election in Rochester, New York. They were arrested, but the case fell apart publicly after the judge made a number of statements against women's rights. Fearing a 'not guilty' verdict, he dismissed the jury and fined Anthony $100. She refused to pay, and the judge – afraid that she would create even more publicity – freed her.

A combination of high-profile events, such as Anthony's trial, exhausting lecture tours and the successful campaign for women's voting rights in Wyoming, helped the cause of woman suffrage. In 1890, the two rival suffrage groups united to form the National American Woman Suffrage Association. Within a few years, Colorado, Utah and Idaho became the first American states to grant women the right to vote. More would follow and, at the same time, the new organization mounted campaigns to change federal voting laws as well.

'Ladies, we must remind ourselves that the weapon of the vote will be for us, just as it is for man, the only means of obtaining the reforms we desire. As long as we remain excluded from **civic** life, men will attend to their own interests rather than to ours.'

French feminist Hubertine Auclert, 1879.

'I think [women] are too hysterical, they are too much disposed to be guided by feeling and not by cold reason, and . . . to refuse any kind of compromise. I do not think that women are safe guides in government, they are very unsafe guides.'

Earl of Halstead, 1907, blocking a bill in Britain's House of Lords that would have granted women limited voting rights.

Britain and Beyond

Suffragists had also been active in Great Britain and its empire. And it was in the empire, rather than in Britain itself, where the first successes occurred. New Zealand granted women the right to vote in 1893, followed ten years later by Australia. Canada would eventually grant women the vote in 1918.

British suffragists faced stronger opposition, both from men in power and from Queen Victoria, who described women's rights as 'mad, wicked folly'. Many British laws and other traditions reflected the old view that men were superior to women. But feminists were firm in their opposition. The British

Emily Davison was killed when she threw herself under a horse during the 1913 Epsom Derby, one of Britain's leading horse races, in order to draw attention to the suffragist movement.

Home Secretary was told that young women were prepared to die for Mrs Emmeline Pankhurst, one of the most ardent British feminists, who pointedly referred to God as a 'She' in her speeches. After British suffragist groups united to form the National Union of Woman Suffrage Societies in 1897, some feminists decided to take extreme action. They turned to **boycotting**, intimidation and bombing to get their message heard. In 1913, one suffragist even threw herself under racehorses at a race attended by the King. Her death sparked national – and international – outrage. But it also showed the lengths to which British women would go to achieve gender equality.

Equality at Last?

The early decades of the 20th century saw eventual victories for the suffrage movements in many countries. British women aged 30 and older gained the right to vote in 1918, and in 1928 this age was lowered to 21 (the same as for men). The state-by-state progress in America led to success on the national level. The 19th Amendment to the US Constitution, passed in 1920, gave women voting rights equal to those of men. Many other countries, including Canada, Germany, and Sweden, passed woman suffrage laws at about the same time. It seemed that women had finally achieved true equality. Or had they?

American women celebrate the passage of the 19th Amendment, just in time for the 1920 presidential election.

Changing Attitudes

Once laws, such as those guaranteeing women the right to vote, are in place, a government must act immediately to ensure that they are enforced. Attitudes are another matter. Throughout the early part of the 20th century, women found that many men, and even some women, believed that now that women had the vote, they should stop 'rocking the boat'.

While many women had hoped that obtaining the vote would be the first step in achieving equality in other

Successes in a 'Man's World'

Examples of women who succeeded in 'men's work' have inspired other girls and women for decades. These successes were particularly important at the beginning of the 20th century, when women faced pressure to remain at home rather than pursue careers. Marie Curie (1867–1934), born Marja Sklodowska in Poland, was the first woman to win the **Nobel Prize** and the first person to win it twice. Her groundbreaking work on **radioactivity**, a term she invented, paved the way for many scientific advances. In 1928, Amelia Earhart (1897–1937) became the first woman to fly across the Atlantic. Four years later, she became the first female transatlantic pilot. She disappeared mysteriously in the middle of an around-the-world flight in 1937. Women were also succeeding in politics. In 1919, the Conservative, Nancy Astor, was elected as Britain's first female MP. Ten years later, Margaret Bondfield became the first female Cabinet member, in the Labour government of Ramsay MacDonald.

areas, they soon found that this was not necessarily the case. Instead of gaining entry into all kinds of work, talented women had very few opportunities to get the training and experience required for many jobs. Despite these difficulties, however, some women did manage to achieve success in science and industry, academia and exploration, and other areas once considered to be part of a 'man's world'. These women struggled to rise to prominence, but their achievements served as examples for future generations.

War Work

The great wave of woman suffrage laws, such as those in the United States and Great Britain, were passed at the end of World War I (1914–18). Many people saw that war, with its millions of soldiers killed in brutal battles, as the last gasp of an old era. They believed that old ways of thinking had made

Besides being the first woman to fly solo across the Atlantic, Amelia Earhart was also the first woman to fly solo nonstop from coast to coast in the US.

23

the war unavoidable and that it was time for a new start. It seemed fitting, as democratic governments replaced many monarchies in Europe, that women should benefit from the changes.

Another global conflict, World War II (1939–45), had an even more profound effect on women's lives around the world. Millions of men had to leave their jobs to fight for their countries. These countries would have ceased to function properly if women had not taken up the jobs that became vacant as a result. Women responded with patriotism and enthusiasm. And for many women, taking a job for the first time gave them an opportunity to earn money for themselves and offered them the first taste of independence.

The jobs that women took were not normally considered 'women's work', such as teaching, nursing and waitressing. Women were now working as engineers, lathe turners and welders in factories. And governments provided facilities that female workers could only have dreamed of before the war, such as nurseries to look after their children.

'I myself have never been able to find out precisely what feminism is; I only know that people call me a feminist whenever I express sentiments that differentiate me from a doormat.'

British author Rebecca West, 1913.

Women's war effort

Early on during World War II, the British and American governments recognized the need to have women filling empty positions in factories. 'Land girls' worked on British farms, while other women filled essential slots in factories producing ammunition and other important supplies. 'Rosie the Riveter' became a familiar face all over the United States, serving as an example to the real women who turned their hands to work.

International Women's Day

The widespread rise of industry in the late 18th and 19th centuries drew many women to work in factories, especially those producing textiles and clothing. Working conditions in these factories were often harsh and, to make matters worse, women were paid less than men. On March 8, 1857, female workers in New England textile factories began a strike, demanding the same pay as that of male workers doing the same job. The strike was successful and inspired many other female workers around the world. In 1910, German feminist Clara Zetkin proposed celebrating March 8 (the anniversary of the beginning of the strike) as International Women's Day. Today, the contributions made by women worldwide are celebrated on this date.

Striking cotton workers demonstrate outside a Chicago factory, demanding a $16 per week minimum wage.

In the UK alone, more than 6.5 million women had become part of the civilian workforce and nearly 500,000 served in the armed forces. Their contribution – like that of women in the United States, the Soviet Union, and other countries – helped earn victory for the Allies. When the war ended in 1945, four out of five of these women wanted to keep their jobs. But would they have their wish?

'Men have singled out women of outstanding merit and put them on a pedestal to avoid recognizing the capabilities of all women.'

Huda Shaarawi, Egyptian writer and women's rights activist, 1924.

Rekindling the Flame

For nearly two decades after the end of World War II, it seemed that the women's liberation movement had come to a stop. Great Britain and many other Western nations entered a period of prosperity. Men reclaimed many of the jobs that women had done during the war. And, with the economy strong, there seemed to be no need for women to work.

Instead of work and independence, women were told that their place was back in the home. Newspaper articles and television commercials told how their lives would be improved with new developments such as frozen foods, along with appliances such as washing machines and dishwashers. Instead of struggling in factories and offices, women could spend time playing bridge or chatting with each other over coffee.

Advertising images from the 1950s showed contented housewives with their modern appliances, but the hidden message was clear – women should stay at home and let men go to work.

Discontent and Protest

But beneath the cosy surface of life in the 1950s and early 1960s, there were serious struggles taking place in many countries. The civil rights movement was developing in the United States. African-Americans and their supporters faced violence and even death in their efforts to achieve racial equality. The US was entering a military involvement in Vietnam, which would eventually lead to widespread anti-war protests. British protesters focused on the rights of nonwhite immigrants and the Catholic minority in Northern Ireland.

Many women were at the forefront of these protests and demonstrations. They were quick to point out that they too still suffered from discrimination and unfair treatment. In an echo from events a century before, when women had helped lead the abolitionist movement, 20th-century feminists found a **common cause** with African-Americans and other minorities.

'As she made the beds, shopped for groceries, ate peanut butter sandwiches with the children, chauffeured Cub Scouts and Brownies . . . she was afraid to ask even of herself the silent question – "Is this all?" '

Betty Friedan, describing the lives of American homemakers in *The Feminine Mystique*, 1963.

New Organizations

The women's movement around the world gained new voices and a new sense of direction in the 1960s. Women were prepared to fight for their rights in the public arena, either as part of wider social issues or by focusing on women-only concerns. The Women's Liberation group set up in Sydney, Australia in 1969 is a good example. Its first public outing was to take part in a rally protesting against Australia's involvement in the US-led war in Vietnam. This involvement raised the profile of the women's movement. National Women's Liberation Conferences, beginning in 1970, concentrated on social and economic issues while paving the way to adding women's concerns to the Australian Labor Party manifesto in the next general election. America's National Organization for Women (NOW) was established in 1966 by women who had inside knowledge of, and experience in national politics. NOW offered feminists the chance to publicize their campaigns and to lobby Congress and other lawmaking bodies in the United States.

A Woman's Place?

Even before the advent of the women's rights movement, women proved that they could succeed in many areas, including those often considered 'man's work'. Queens such as Nefertiti of Egypt or England's Elizabeth I ruled their lands with skill and power. Joan of Arc was a remarkable military leader, and Florence Nightingale opened many doors in the field of medicine.

These women's accomplishments were all the more remarkable because they succeeded at a time when women were thought to be less capable than men. Opportunities grew when conditions for women improved – largely as a result of having the vote – at the beginning of the 20th century.

Newfound Strength

By the 1960s, with feminism becoming more of a force, women were able to stretch their capabilities even further. Not only did they use their vote, but they also began to be elected to political office. Some women rose to become national leaders in their countries (see page 33). Others challenged traditional boundaries in sports, entertainment and business.

Queen Elizabeth I of Bohemia, sister of England's King Charles I, needed courage and diplomacy to rule during the turbulent 17th century.

Sporting Triumphs

Women have been making their presence felt in organized sports for more than a century. In 1928, Gertrude Ederle became the first woman to swim the English Channel, and women first took part in gymnastics and athletics events at the Olympic Games. Other sports have also opened their doors to women. British women's football clubs have competed for a national trophy since 1970. The Football Association took over the competition in the 1993–4 season, with 147 clubs entering. Since then, the FA Women's Challenge Cup Final has become a popular fixture and a record 13,824 spectators saw Arsenal defeat Fulham in the 2001 final. And in 1996, one of the most masculine of all barriers came crashing down when Cristina Sanchez became Spain's first female bullfighter.

The US Women's soccer team celebrates after beating Brazil 2–1 to win the gold medal at the Athens Olympic Games, 2004. Girls and women have led the way in popularizing soccer in the US.

First Woman in Space

While most of the high-profile demonstrations for gender equality were in the Western world in the 20th century, communist countries were eager to demonstrate that their women already received equal treatment. The Soviet Union used its highly publicized space exploration program to do just that. On June 16, 1963, Valentina Tereshkova (1937–) was launched into space, orbiting Earth 48 times in just under three days. After returning, she travelled to other countries as a **goodwill ambassador** and received a standing ovation at the United Nations (UN). Tereshkova's flight proved what Soviet scientists had predicted: women were able to withstand the stresses of space travel just as well as men were.

Of course, these successes benefited those who were directly involved by giving them more power and responsibility. But, just as importantly, they acted as examples for future generations of girls. Girls could now find examples of leading women scientists, politicians, artists and sports stars. The hope these women offered was as important – if not more so – than any laws guaranteeing equal rights between the genders.

Healing the World

Australian **paediatrician** Dr Helen Caldicott has been an example for women in many areas of life. After establishing an international reputation for the treatment of **cystic fibrosis**, she turned her attention to the subject of nuclear disarmament. Like many women before her, she believed that the worst threats to world peace came from the male-dominated military systems in many countries. In the 1970s, she founded Physicians for Social Responsibility (PSR) and Women's Action for Nuclear Disarmament. Dr Caldicott's persuasive public appearances and books gained enormous publicity. A film based on her book *Eight Minutes to Midnight* won the Academy Award for best documentary in 1983. Two years later, the international branch of PSR received the Nobel Peace Prize.

Feminist and peace activist Dr Helen Caldicott (centre) poses with actresses Meryl Streep (left) and Jill Clayburgh (right) in the 1980s.

'I read *The Female Eunuch* by Germaine Greer – a wonderful Australian woman. She said, look, you don't have to do what people tell you to do. You don't have to be what society says, you can be yourself. It gave me such a sense of power.'

Dr Helen Caldicott, describing how she was inspired to campaign for world peace.

Mothers of the Disappeared

From 1976 to 1982, Argentina was ruled by a military **dictatorship**. The country's leaders imprisoned or executed thousands of people, often without trial. These were people that the government considered 'dangerous' or 'troublemakers'. Another 30,000 simply disappeared without a trace. Most Argentine people were too afraid of the military death squads to protest, but a group of brave women did just that in the heart of the capital, Buenos Aires. The 'Mothers of the Disappeared' began their protest on April 30, 1977. This women-only group maintained a presence outside the Government House (the seat of the government) until civilian rule was restored in 1983. Their actions inspired other women's groups in Latin America and beyond. In 1985, a group of Iranian mothers met some of the former Argentine demonstrators to form a similar group in their own country.

Women Take Charge

As women around the world continue to use their vote – both to influence governments and to be elected themselves – some women have become national leaders. Sirimavo Ratwatte Dias Bandaranaike (1916–2000) was prime minister of Ceylon (now Sri Lanka) from 1960 to 1965, 1970 to 1977 and 1994 to 2000. In 1966, Indira Gandhi (1917–74) became prime minister of India, the

Indira Gandhi became prime minister of India two years after the country's first prime minister – her father, Jawaharlal Nehru – died in 1964.

largest democracy in the world. Margaret Thatcher (1925–) became prime minister in the UK in 1979 and she went on to win two more elections. Other modern female leaders have included Corazon Aquino (1933–) in the Philippines, Benazir Bhutto (1953–) in Pakistan, Kim Campbell (1947–) in Canada and Tansu Çiller (1946–) in Turkey.

Feminism as a Force

Since the early 1970s, the goals of feminists and others campaigning for gender equality have widened. New laws in many countries have enshrined the idea of equality in pay, banking, education and many other areas. But, just as activists succeed in one area, other issues arise. It is one thing, for example, to earn the same as a man for a similar job. It is another to be able to afford the childcare that many women need to take the job in the first place. And it is another issue altogether to ensure that a woman's job will still be there when she returns after having a baby and taking maternity leave.

As so often before, progress for women was tied in with, or followed on from, progress in other social issues. In 1968, Leonora Lloyd (1940–2002) helped set up Britain's Joint Action Committee for Women's Equal Rights. The trigger was

Feminists at a New York rally celebrating six decades of woman suffrage, turn their attention to the Equal Rights Amendment, 1980.

The Movement is the Message

While some people have been disappointed by what they have seen as slow progress towards gender equality, others have seen the movement itself as a success. Feminism is no longer confined to a few well-educated, wealthy women. The sense of solidarity forged in the struggle has inspired girls and women from all backgrounds.

Feminism has a great deal of potential. As a movement, it has drawn strength from the different individuals and groups that have played a part in improving women's conditions worldwide. Strength in numbers, coupled with strength in **diversity**, has given the campaign for gender equality a foundation.

Some feminists have used their skills as writers to highlight the injustices faced by women and the remedies they propose to overcome them. Others believe that 'shock tactics' are the best way to shake people from old ways of thinking. Still others believe that women need to have the financial or political power to make necessary changes themselves.

Nancy Pelosi, leader of the Democratic Party in the US House of Representatives, addresses a special political lunch supporting woman candidates during the Democratic Convention in Boston, 2004.

a bitter strike among Ford Motor workers, concerned about the principle of equal pay for work of equal value. This principle was central to the Equal Pay Act, which became law in 1970.

Florence Kelley, who campaigned for better pay and working conditions for American women during World War I

Backed by the Law

The most dramatic legal advance in gender equality occurred when women were granted the right to vote. The campaign, however, had always been much broader than that single issue. Some of the most far-reaching progress has come in the workplace. The first conference of Britain's Women's Liberation movement, in 1970, resolved to concentrate on economic advances. Their campaigning soon bore fruit. The Equal Pay and Sex Discrimination Act took effect in Great Britain in 1975. Britain established the Equal Opportunities Commission – to monitor working practices – at the same time. Later Acts, such as the Employment rights Act of 1994 enshrined in law principles such as maternity leave (paid time off to have a baby).

After many long-fought campaigns, the first US measures were the Equal Pay Act and the Sex Discrimination Act (both passed in 1963), which promised the same pay for the same work for women and men.

Attacking Miss World

Many people believe that female beauty contests are more harmful than they might seem. These critics argue that the contests strengthen society's view that women can hope only to be beautiful, not successful in other fields. The participants in beauty contests, these critics argue, are simply objects for men's pleasure.

In 1970, a group of 25 feminists took these criticisms a step farther at the Miss World competition in London. Millions of television viewers worldwide watched as, at a given signal, the protesters got out of their seats and charged the stage. They threw stink bombs and exploding bags of flour. Some of the protesters even used squirt guns to shoot entertainer Bob Hope, the host of the event, before being ushered off the stage by security guards. One of the protesters later said, 'We wanted to get across the idea that there was more to women than their vital statistics'.

Pat Carbine (left) and Glora Steinem, co-founders of Ms. Magazine, *pose in front of a special anniversary issue of the publication.*

Word is Out

An explosion of new writing helped the cause of feminists in the early 1970s. Two important books, *The Female Eunuch* by Australian feminist Germaine Greer and *The Second Sex* by French scholar Simone de Beauvoir, were published in 1970. *Ms. Magazine* was first published as an insert in *New York* magazine in 1971; 300,000 copies sold out in eight days. Its co-founder, Gloria Steinem, went on to edit the magazine, turning it into an important source of news about women's rights. *Spare Rib*, a magazine with similar goals, began publishing in 1972 in Great Britain. And in 1973, Carmen Calil launched Virago, the first feminist publishing house, in Great Britain.

Unfinished Business

Although the focus of the gender equality campaign has shifted over the years, a number of core gender issues have remained at the forefront, where some of them have been for more than a century. One of these issues is how women can control their bodies and their choices about whether or not to have children. And despite equal opportunity laws in many countries, women still face a **glass ceiling** in many professions.

Powerful Opposition

Activists for gender equality have faced fierce and vocal opposition for many decades. In the early days of the abolitionist movement, well-qualified women were denied the opportunity to speak at public meetings, even by the men who relied on their support and planning skills. Suffragists were heckled and mocked at meetings. One leading American suffragist, Susan B. Anthony, even carried a pistol to public meetings because she had been threatened so many times.

By the 1990s, more men were willing to take on childcare and household responsibilities.

The Equal Rights Amendment

One of the most long-standing – and still unfinished – feminist campaigns involves the Equal Rights Amendment in the United States. This proposed amendment to the US Constitution was drafted by women's rights activist Alice Paul in 1923, just three years after American women gained the right to vote. The wording seemed harmless, simply reaffirming the rights that should apply to all US citizens: 'Equality of rights under the law shall not be denied or abridged by the United States or by any State on account of sex'.

The proposal was submitted to each session of Congress (the first step before it would go to each state to be ratified, or approved) from 1923 to 1972, when it was finally approved. Then it had to be ratified by 38 states (two-thirds of the total) before it could become an Amendment. A deadline for ratification, imposed by Congress, was extended to 1982 but at that time the bill had been approved by only 35 states.

The ERA is once more, as it was before 1972, being reintroduced to each session of Congress. The latest version includes provisions for gay rights; it also sets no deadline for ratification by the states.

Besides drafting the first ERA, Alice Paul organized several militant protests and rallies in support of women's rights.

Attitudes change slowly and, even in an age when most people accept women's rights, there are those who continue to criticize and cause trouble. Modern opponents often take issue with what is called 'political correctness', a way of speaking and writing that is careful not to offend women or minorities who once faced discrimination. Like many moves to change people's attitudes, political correctness can be taken to extremes. Critics often point to these extremes, without acknowledging that most new terms (such as 'police officer' in place of 'policeman') work just as well as the old terms, without favouring one gender.

In countries where women have achieved greater equality, other concerns have arisen. Some men have viewed each increase in women's rights as a loss to the privileged position that they believe men should have in society. That view, however misguided, can have tragic consequences, as in the case of the Montreal Massacre (see panel). Supporters of gender equality need to make it clear that greater equality benefits all of society, not just part of it.

The 'Montreal Massacre'

Throughout the history of the campaign for gender equality, women have faced a backlash from people (usually men) who oppose change. On December 6, 1989, the world learned of a massacre in Montreal, Canada, that was linked to such a backlash. Marc Lépine, a local man, entered the Ecole Polytechnique, one of Canada's leading engineering schools. Waving a rifle, he separated the men from the women, screaming about how he hated feminists.
Lepine then began to shoot, killing 14 women (13 students and a secretary) before turning the gun on himself and committing suicide. Lepine left a note blaming feminists for ruining his life.

Canadian Prime Minister Jean Chretien commemorates the 10th anniversary of the Montreal Massacre, 1999.

The massacre shocked Canada, prompting new measures in gun control and about violence against women. December 6 is now observed as a memorial day to mark the nation's worst mass murder.

Our Bodies, Ourselves

One of the most controversial areas of gender equality involves pregnancy. Social reformers in the 19th century felt that women needed to have more control over how often they became pregnant in order to ensure their health, as well as the health of their children. For nearly two centuries, feminists have campaigned for birth control, **contraception**, and **abortion** rights. A 1973 book called *Our Bodies, Ourselves* argued that women should have the right to decide how to deal with their bodies and having children. Great Britain (in 1967) and the United States (in 1973) made abortion legal. However, many people see abortion as a religious issue rather than a gender equality issue, and many anti-abortion groups have campaigned to make the practice illegal again. Abortion remains illegal in many other countries.

Many feminists believe that men have no right to interfere on issues that they can never experience.

'When the government starts targeting individual groups for legalized discrimination, every woman's rights are at stake.'

NOW President, Kim Gandy, September 2002, supporting the vote in Miami-Dade County, Florida, to oppose discrimination against gay and lesbian citizens.

Gender inequality still lingers in the workplace in most countries. In 2003, the average earnings of female workers in Britain were 19 per cent lower than those of men.

77% of anti-abortion leaders are men. 100% of them will never be pregnant.

It's your body. It's your decision. The Pro-Choice Public Education Project. It's pro-choice or no choice.
1-888/253-CHOICE or www.protectchoice.org

Looking Ahead

The campaign for gender equality entered the 21st century with a long history of struggle behind it but with some notable successes as well. Conditions for women have been improving in many countries, and women have been able to influence the course of politics more successfully. But many areas of the world, including parts of Africa and the Middle East, remain locked in social systems that deny basic equality to women. The focus in this new century has begun to turn towards these countries.

The Wider View

Some societies interpret their religions and cultural traditions in ways that discriminate against women. Too often, age-old customs have been based on poorly understood interpretations of religious guidelines. The Koran, the holy book of Islam, makes it clear that women have the same worth as men.

Yet many Islamic countries still deny women basic rights. Some interpretations of Christianity, Judaism and Hinduism take a similar view.

Veiled Muslim women take part in Afghanistan's first direct presidential election in October 2004.

Tanzanian students have benefited from the country's increased emphasis on education.

Education for All

The different organizations run by the United Nations try to promote basic rights around the globe. The United Nations Educational, Scientific and Cultural Organization (UNESCO) has singled out gender equality as one of its main challenges in the first decades of the 21st century. Its ambitious Education for All (EFA) program has targeted schooling as the best way to meet this challenge.

The EFA has two main goals. The first, originally given a deadline of 2005, is to promote gender equality in enrolment, making sure that girls have the same rights to attend school as boys. Funds from UNESCO can help put this into practice. The second goal – with a target date of 2015 – is to develop equality of achievement. This broader goal involves making sure that girls have the same access to learning materials within the classroom as boys do. At the same time, girls and boys are shown examples of successful women in a way that should inspire both groups to achieve their best.

Overcoming such obstacles is difficult because reformers do not want to appear to be interfering with other people's cultures. But the world at large can make a difference by supporting projects to increase **literacy** and reduce poverty. By helping people, especially women, learn to improve their own condition, the world can help ideas of equality develop on their own in places where they were once denied.

Empowerment

The word 'empowerment' has become a rallying cry for many people striving to develop long-lasting equality – and not simply gender equality. It ties in with the long tradition of building new systems from the ground up, rather than imposing them on people. For example, an international aid group might provide a poor village in a developing country with better irrigation, modern farming equipment, fertilizer and seeds. The village farmers are **empowered** because they now have the means to improve their own condition.

Empowerment is important for gender equality in many ways. Generally, girls and women are empowered when educational and work-related obstacles are removed or when they see examples of successful women. Changed attitudes about what a girl can hope to do can empower her to follow her ambitions.

One practical success story is still underway in the Asian country of Nepal, where women traditionally had little say in managing their own financial affairs. The Women's Empowerment Program (WEP) has focused on literacy as the key to improving women's conditions. WEP literacy programs have, in slightly more than three years, helped triple the number of Nepali women who can read and write. In addition, the program has used loans to help women set up businesses that they can run themselves. As a result, the number of women involved in businesses has risen from 19,000 to 86,000, and their earnings have gone from $1.2 million to more than $10 million.

'We still need a philosophy to guide us on this journey of change: a philosophy that is not pro-woman (or pro-man) but pro-fairness that stresses flexibility and more options for all.'

Cathy Young, Russian-born writer, in her essay 'Ceasefire! Why Women and Men Must Join Forces to Achieve True Equality', 1999.

Emily's List

In 1985, 25 politically active American women started a network to raise money for women running for political office. They called this network Emily's List. The name Emily is an acronym for the saying 'Early Money Is Like Yeast – it raises dough'. Organizers send information about candidates to members of the List and these people can then send donations to candidates of their choice. Emily's List concentrates on supporting female candidates who support the cause of gender equality. By 2004, Emily's List had helped elect 11 US Senators, 55 Congresswomen and seven state governors.

Women's involvement in the British political system has also become headline news. One of the reasons for Tony Blair's landslide victory in 1997 was the number of female parliamentary candidates (nicknamed 'Blair's Babes'), and the interest they created among voters. Overnight, the number of women MPs nearly doubled from 63 to 122. The Conservative and Liberal Democrat parties took note and have since opened the door to more female prospective parliamentary candidates.

A Show of Strength

The campaign for gender equality has often taken its case directly to those who have power, whether at the seat of national government, local authority offices or even a local town hall. On October 15, 2000, thousands of people around the world took part in the World March of Women 2000. Women's groups representing a wide range of concerns united to focus on two important issues – violence against women and women's equality. Protestors also noted how tackling world poverty would benefit women; more than two-thirds of the world's population lives in poverty, and women make up 70 per cent of this total. Speakers addressed the peaceful demonstrators who gathered outside the UN headquarters in New York, outside the Houses of Parliament in London, by the White House in Washington, DC, and in dozens of other national and international centres.

Glossary and Suggested Reading

abortion   a medical operation to end a pregnancy

Age of Enlightenment   a time when there were many new ideas about society and science

blue-collar   related to work using the hands, as opposed to office (white-collar) work

boycotting   refusing to do business with a person or company as a form of protest

charter   a written document outlining the goals of an organization or country

civic   relating to government

civil rights   basic human rights ensuring that all citizens receive the same treatment

common cause   points of agreement between two people or groups

communism   a type of government in which the state (government) owns all properties and businesses

contraception   a method of preventing a pregnancy from occurring

convention   a gathering of people with a shared goal

cystic fibrosis   a life-threatening disease of the lungs and digestive system

dictatorship   an undemocratic form of government in which a single ruler has virtually total control over a country

discrimination   treating people poorly because of their appearance, behaviour, or background

diversity   a wide range of qualities

empowered   given more chance to develop, either through laws or from the example of others

feminist   supporting the rights of women, or a person who strongly supports these rights

glass ceiling   an unofficial barrier that stops certain people from rising within an organization (they can see up to what they want but cannot pass through the ceiling)

goodwill ambassador   a respected person who travels widely to promote support for an organization

guillotine   a device used to execute people by cutting off their heads with a sliding blade

humanism   a belief in the good qualities and potential of human beings

illiteracy   inability to read and write

interest   extra money charged on the repayment of money that is borrowed

lash   a whip

literacy   ability to read and write

lobby   to seek support for a cause within a government

minority groups   groups of people with some shared qualities (such as language, skin colour or religion) who make up less than half of a larger population

Nobel Prize   an award for excellence in science or another subject

paediatrician   a doctor specializing in the care of children

Playboy bunnies   women who dress in skimpy costumes to entertain men at nightclubs

radioactivity   a type of energy, sometimes dangerous, that occurs in nature

Reformation   the period of Christian history, beginning in the early 16th century, when some people sought to change (reform) the beliefs and practices of the Catholic Church

reincarnated   reborn in a different body

revolutions   violent overthrow of countries or political systems

scaffold   a platform from which condemned people were hanged

subjugation   a condition with very few individual freedoms

territory   in the United States, an area that does not have enough population to become a state but that can still govern itself in many ways

Western   countries that rejected communism and allowed individuals to own businesses and property

Suggested Reading

Stearman, Kaye. *Ideas of the Modern World: Feminism.* London: Hodder, 2005.

Atkinson, Diane. *Votes for Women.* Cambridge: Cambridge University Press, 1988.

Stearman, Kaye. *Women's Rights: Changing Attitudes 1900—2000.* London: Wayland and Amnesty International, 1999.

Trioli, Virginia. *Generation f: sex, power and the young feminist.* Port Melbourne, Australia: Minerva, 1996

Web sites

Emmeline Pankhurst – British Suffage Leader

www.womenshistory.about.com/ od/suffrageengland/p/pankhurst.htm

Spartacus Educational Site

www.spartacus.schoolnet.co.uk

'Votes for Women' Suffrage Pictures (Library of Congress)

http://lcweb2.loc.gov/ammem/vfwhtml/vfwhome.html

Mary Wollstonecraft

http://www.galegroup.com/free_resources/whm/bio/wollstonecraft_m.htm

Australian Electoral History: Milestones for Women

http://www.aec.gov.au/_content/When/history/milestones.htm

Index